Usui Reiki Level II

A COMPLETE GUIDE TO THE HOLISTIC HEALING MODALITY

USUI REIKI – LEVEL 2

Djamel Boucly

© **Copyright 2015 - All rights reserved.**
In no way is it legal to reproduce, duplicate, or transmit any part of this document in either electronic means or in printed format. Recording of this publication is strictly prohibited and any storage of this document is not allowed unless with written permission from the publisher. All rights reserved.

The information provided herein is stated to be truthful and consistent, in that any liability, in terms of inattention or otherwise, by any usage or abuse of any policies, processes, or directions contained within is the solitary and utter responsibility of the recipient reader. Under no circumstances will any legal responsibility or blame be held against the publisher for any reparation, damages, or monetary loss due to the information herein, either directly or indirectly.

Respective authors own all copyrights not held by the publisher.

Author's Disclaimer:
Although Reiki offers a variety of benefits and is practiced all over the world today, the material in this manual should not be considered to override any diagnosis made by a Qualified Doctor or Specialist. But, it can be considered as an additional form of treatment. The author cannot accept any responsibility for any illness arising out of the failure of the reader and/or student, to seek medical advice from a Qualified Doctor or Specialist.

Important note to the Student/Reader:
The purpose of this manual is to offer the reader insight to the teachings and disciplines associated with First Degree Usui Reiki. The information in this manual has been derived from the traditional teachings of Dr. Mikao Usui and does not contain any of the Authors personal beliefs and or practices.
In order to use this manual to heal yourself or others, you must first receive the necessary Reiki attunements from a Reiki Master

Table of Contents

Usui Reiki Level II 1
Practitioners Ethics 4
Reiki Symbols 7
Energy Protection and Space Clearing 19
Healing Techniques 23
Smoothing/Un-ruffling the Aura 29
Beaming 33
Client Relations 37
Distant Healing 59
Chakra Affirmations 63
Healing with Color 67
Healing with Sound 71
Manifestation 81
Psychic Development 87
Final Thoughts 93
Interesting References 110

INTRODUCTION

Practitioners Ethics

There are three levels of training in Usui Reiki. Level 1 focuses on you - the student, in order to heal yourself. Level 1 has to be completed, before moving on to Level 2, after which you are permitted to offer Reiki as an alternative form of healing to others, as a Practitioner.

With this knowledge also comes responsibility. You have a responsibility towards yourself and those who choose to seek you out for healing.

Ethics

- Honour yourself, your practice and Reiki energy. Practice the 5 precepts (Gokai) daily. This will aid you in being an ethical and compassionate Practitioner.

For today only:

Do not anger – Ikaruna

Do not worry – Shinpai Suna

With thankfulness – Kansha Shite

Work diligently – Gyo Wo Hageme

Be kind to others – Hito Ni Shinsetsu Ni

- A Reiki Practitioner may not make a medical diagnosis. You may not prescribe or advise a client to discontinue any medication and/or medical treatment prescribed by a professional Doctor, Specialist or any Medical Practitioner.

- You may never "force" Reiki on anyone. Do not impose your will on anyone who does not choose to have a Reiki healing (out of their own free will).

- Do not promise an outcome of a healing session. The outcome of a healing session is not within your control – healing is based on what the client requires. Remember that Reiki energy will go where it needs to go and do what it needs to do. The client's higher self will take from the healing session whatever is required from the session.

- Practice confidentiality. A Practitioner must act with integrity and you should therefore keep the details of a session confidential.

- Being a Reiki Practitioner does not grant you a higher level of spiritual standing above anyone else. Remember the precept "Be kind to others" - You have to remain loving and compassionate towards all living beings.

- Do not denounce other healers and their healing modalities. Every healer has his/her own unique gift and we will all express our purpose in a unique manner.

CHAPTER 1

Reiki Symbols

There are three main Reiki symbols, which we will cover in this manual. Many Reiki Masters believe that the Reiki symbols should be kept secret from anyone outside of the Reiki network and should only be passed down from Reiki Master to the student/practitioner. Although the Reiki symbols are sacred, they are certainly not a secret.

The symbols hold very little power outside of the ability of the Practitioner and they are mainly used as a tool to activate a specific energy for healing. They serve as a key to open the higher consciousness and unlock specific energy systems. The power lies not in the symbol itself, but rather in what the symbol represents.

When a student is attuned to the Reiki symbols, the components of the symbol is imprinted in the students mind and merges with the energies which they each represent. When the Practitioner visualizes, draws or thinks about a symbol, it will instantly connect him/her to the energies that the symbol represents.

There are different forms of Reiki today and some have incorporated their own symbols into their attunements. However, in "traditional" Reiki, three Reiki symbols are given during the Level 2 attunement.
These symbols are as follows:

- Cho Ku Rei – The power symbol
- Sei He Ki – The mental and emotional symbol
- Hon Sha Ze Sho Nen – The distance symbol

Cho Ku Rei

The Power Symbol

This is the power symbol. Pronounced "cha-coo-ray", which means "Place the power of the universe here". It is used to activate Reiki energy.

1) The horizontal line represents the Reiki source, also known as the God line.

2) The vertical line represents the energy flow – the hara line.
3) The spiral, which touches the vertical (centre) line seven times, represents the seven (main) chakras.

This symbol focuses, boosts and also amplifies Reiki energy. It is also used (first) to amplify the other Reiki symbols. At the end of a Reiki treatment session you will use Cho Ku Rei to seal in the Reiki energy.

This is done by drawing the symbol just above the recipient's Solar Plexus Chakra and then putting your hand over it (to seal the energy in).

- This symbol signifies the power of three – Divine Perfection. (The Son, the Father and the Holy Ghost).

- The number 7 - Relating to the seven chakras, is the number of Spiritual Perfection.

- The number 10 - Is the number of Ordinal Perfection. It relates to the relationship between spirit and matter, ordinance and /or divine structure. Ordinal structure, in other words control over chaos.

- The number 12 - Is in charge of Governmental Laws. It signifies the twelve Disciples. There are also twelve "special" beads found in a rosary.

To activate this symbol, you need to visualize the symbol, physically draw the symbol or say its name three times. Numbers also have a significant meaning in the practice of Reiki.

Sei He Ki

The Mental and Emotional Symbol

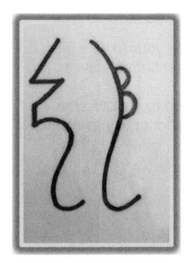 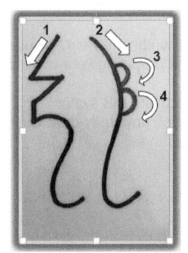

This is the mental and emotional symbol. Pronounced "say-he-key", which means "God and man become one" or "as is above, so is below".

This symbol balances the left and right hemispheres of the brain, ultimately bringing the body and mind together. This symbol also signifies peace and harmony.

This symbol may be used to heal relationship problems, emotional and/or mental distress, such as depression, fear, anxiety loss and addictions etc.

- This symbol signifies the key to the universe.

- It also signifies the balance between God and man, when God and man became one.

- Balance ultimately = Harmony.

This symbol may also be used on your food, either whilst preparing your meal or just before you eat.

To activate this symbol, you need to visualize the symbol, physically draw the symbol or say its name three times.

Hon Sha Ze Sho Nen

The Distant Healing Symbol

 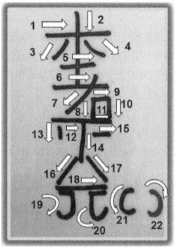

This is the distant healing symbol. Pronounced "hon-sha-zee-show-nen", which means "no past, no present, no future". It can also mean "the Buddha in me contacts the Buddha in you".

As the name symbolizes, it can be used to send energy over a distance. When using this symbol, time and distance has no effect on the Reiki energy that is sent.
This symbol is also used in karmic healing, including trauma and other emotions we experience in this lifetime. It allows emotions from previous or parallel

lives, which affect and mirror people's behaviour, to be brought to the surface, to be released.

- This symbol signifies "timelessness".

- It also signifies "the light in me, is the light in you".

- This symbol can be used to send Reiki energy (healing) to anyone, anywhere in the world, at any time, as this symbol is not affected by time and distance.

This symbol may also be used on your food, either whilst preparing your meal or just before you eat.

To activate this symbol, you need to visualize the symbol, physically draw the symbol or say its name three times.

Practice makes perfect! So, try this exercise – draw each Reiki symbol and write down its meaning and uses. Repeat this exercise three times.

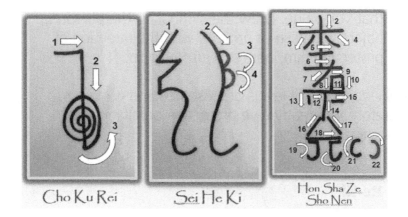

Cho Ku Rei   Sei He Ki   Hon Sha Ze Sho Nen

Reiki Symbols – Additional Uses

Cho Ku Rei

- You can use this symbol on any specific part of the body (i.e. where you may be experiencing pain). Draw the symbol on the specific area that you are planning to treat.
- You can use this symbol to active and boost manifestation.
- You can use this symbol to cleanse crystals and other objects of negative energy. Draw the symbol on or over the crystal or object, with the intention of cleansing it and restoring it to its original state. You can hold the crystal or object in your hands and channel Reiki to it.
- You can protect your energy, your spouse, your children, your home, your vehicle or anything else

that you value. Draw the symbol on the person or object you wish to protect, with the intention of protecting him, her (or it) from harm.

Reiki works on all levels of existence and will therefore inherently give protection on all levels of existence.

Sei He Ki

- You can use this symbol to close tears in the aura, after surgery and anaesthetic.
- You can use this symbol, to assist in weight loss.
- You can use this symbol to find lost items, such as your house keys etc. Let go of trying to find the missing object. Draw the symbol in front of you and ask for help in finding the item. *The answer will soon come to you.*
- You can use this symbol to assist your memory when you are studying, or reading. Draw the symbol on the page that you are busy reading, with the intention of remembering the important parts/information.

Hon Sha Ze Sho Nen

- You can use this symbol to send Reiki energy to a specific task or situation i.e. if you are going for an important job interview, or you may be starting a new job, or if you are going for an operation etc.
- You can use this symbol to heal the past, or understand and release past trauma.
- You can use this symbol over your food or drink water, in conjunction with Sei He Ki. This will increase the nutritional value and purify the water.

CHAPTER 2

Energy Protection and Space Clearing

Apart from using these symbols for the purpose of healing, you will also use them to activate and protect your energy system and to clear your personal and healing space. Therefore, these symbols will become a part of your daily life.

Energy Protection

1. Stand with your feet hip width apart.
2. Ground your energy, with the grounding meditation and call on your Guides and Angels.
3. Then say Cho Ku Rei three times and draw the symbol on the palm of your hand and tap the palm three times (to activate Reiki energy).
4. Then proceed to seal your seven main chakras – cup your hand and place it over the Chakra. *(Repeat this with each Chakra).*
5. Start with your Root Chakra.
6. Repeat step three and seal the Sacral Chakra.
7. Repeat step three and seal the Solar Plexus.

8. Repeat step three and seal the Heart Chakra.
9. Repeat step three and seal the Throat Chakra.
10. Repeat step three and seal the Third Eye Chakra
11. Repeat step three and seal the Crown Chakra.
12. Then draw a big Cho Ku Rei in front of you and lift your hand in the air and pull your arm back over your head, all the way down to the ground. This is to protect the back of your aura.

Space Clearing

1. Stand with your feet hip width apart.
2. Ground your energy, with the grounding meditation and call on your Guides and Angels.
3. As you say Cho Ku Rei three times - use your whole hand or only your index and middle fingers to draw the power symbol (in the air) in front of you.
4. Visualize that the symbol is duplicated five times (as if you have made carbon copies).
5. Physically point your hand or index and middle fingers at the symbol and (move) and place the symbol in each corner of the room and above (in the centre) of the room (as if in a pyramid effect).
6. Repeat this in all the Reiki symbols.

7. Ask your Guides and Angels to assist you to clear and cleanse the room and to fill the room with healing and loving energy.

Image obtained from Pixabay (September 2016)

Remember to trust yourself and your ability. Do not allow self-doubt to mar your progress... and enjoy the journey!

CHAPTER 3

Healing Techniques

Scanning with your hands (Byôsen)

Set your intention to scan the energy. Cup your hands and start at the head and slowly move your hands over the body (approximately 5cm above the body). Pay attention to any responses you may feel in your hands.

You may come across an area where there is a blockage in the energy – in this area you may feel heat, cold, tingling or you may experience other sensations in your hands. You may advise the client of this area and allow him or her to advise or describe whether he or she has any symptoms.

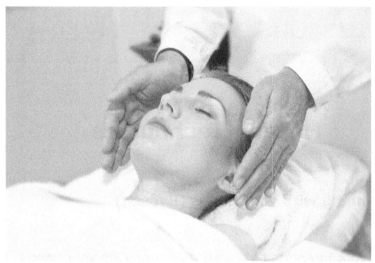
Image obtained from Pixabay (September 2016)

Trust your intuition, do not doubt your abilities.

Scanning with a Pendulum

Set your intention to scan the energy. Gently hold the pendulum between your index and middle fingers and lower it into the chakra areas, one at a time and observe the pendulum's responses.

With a pendulum you can only ask for a clear "yes" or "no", to allow you into the person's energy. The pendulum will pick up on the person's energy.

If the pendulum swings in a clockwise motion, it indicates a healthy chakra (open and balanced). If the pendulum swings in an anti-clockwise motion it indicates an unhealthy chakra – it is taking in energy and not pushing energy out. This is an indication of an emotional disturbance.

If the pendulum is still and not moving at all this indicates that the chakra is closed. There is an energy blockage in that particular chakra.

A pendulum can also be used to indicate the size of a chakra – if the pendulum swings in a small circular (clockwise) motion, it indicates that the chakra is small and the bigger the circle, the bigger the chakra.

As a fun experiment, you can use a pendulum to indicate the size of your palm chakras, by gently holding the pendulum slightly above the palm of your hand.

Selenite Pendulum

Image obtained from Pixabay (September 2016)

Scanning with Crystals

Set your intention to scan the energy. Use a clear quartz terminator and move the point slowly through the energy field in a clockwise motion.

Pay attention to the sensations you may experience in certain areas, i.e. where the crystal feels heavier. This is an indication that there is a lot of energy moving or there may be an energy blockage.

It may also feel as if the crystal wants to move in an alternative direction etc. Pay attention to the different sensations and follow your intuition.

Trust your intuition – It will never misguide you!

Clear Quarts Terminator

Image obtained from Pixabay (September 2016)

CHAPTER 4

Smoothing/Un-ruffling the Aura

The aura normally appears denser in an area where there is pain, stress or an energy blockage i.e. higher density over the head, neck and shoulders, if the person is experiencing pain, due to muscle spasm and/or postural pain in this area.

The reason for smoothing or un-ruffling the aura, is to ensure that the energy is evenly redistributed throughout the energy system. There are two techniques which you may use to do this:

1. Place your one hand on the client's naval (power area) and use the other hand to smooth or un-ruffle the aura.
2. Alternatively, you may use both hands to smooth or un-ruffle the aura.

You may use whichever method you feel most comfortable with.

Smoothing / Un-ruffling the Aura

Using both hands

- Cup your hands (palms facing the client).
- Gently start above the crown, moving your hands in a gentle, but deliberate circular motion, moving your hands inward towards the "centre line".
- Follow the centre line, from the crown all the way down the body (towards the feet).
- Flick off excess energy at the client's hands and feet.
- Continue the movement past the client's feet.

- Then repeat this process along each side of the client's body.

CHAPTER 5

Beaming

Beaming can be used in instances where hands-on healing is not possible, i.e. with burn victims, where the person cannot be touched or where touch would cause pain.

It may also be used where there is a threat of infection (either to the healer or the recipient), as well as in cases of abuse, where the recipient is reluctant to be touched.

Reiki practitioners also use this technique, when working with large animals.

Beaming can also be used at the beginning or end of a treatment, as it increases the energy flow in the client's aura, as it slowly penetrates the client's body. You may also beam energy into an area where the client is experiencing pain.

How to Beam Energy

- Stand approximately 1 to 2 metres away from the client (outside of the client's aura).
- Activate the Distant Dealing Symbol - Hon Sha Ze Sho Nen.
- Then use both hands facing the client and beam Reiki energy into the client's aura.
- Begin at the crown (head) and move down the body, to the feet.
- Beam Reiki energy to both sides of the client's body.

Removing an Energy Blockage

"Reiki First Aid"

Scooping (also referred to as scraping). This techniques is used to remove negative or stagnant energy, which has become lodged in the client's energy system.

This technique should be used in moderation. It can be used for the following:

- To remove severe pain.
- To alleviate stress.

- For Infection.
- To alleviate pain caused by inflammation.
- To remove an energy blockage (here you would notice highly heated areas).
- For depression (but one has to be cautious when treating someone who suffers from depression).

Allow your intuition to guide you whether to use scooping and how much energy to scoop. However, you should bear in mind that this may be uncomfortable for a person with a very sensitive energy system. Rather avoid scooping on sensitive energy systems.

Scooping negative/stagnant energy

- Scoop negative or stagnant energy from the client's energy systems, by suing both hands (as you would scoop handfuls of sand or flour).
- Flick this energy from your hands, into the flame of a candle. (Fire is considered a very powerful transformer of energy).
- Once the energy blockage has been removed, set the intention to fill the area with healing, loving energy and place both your hands (your palms) over the scooped area.
- Do this for as long as you are guided to do so.
- Once you feel that the area has been filled, smooth over the aura, draw the Cho Ku Rei

symbol over the area and seal in the new purified energy.

Image obtained from Pixabay (September 2016)

CHAPTER 6

Client Relations

As a Reiki practitioner, you will be sought out by those in need of physical, emotional, spiritual or mental healing. Healing can bring various supressed emotions to the surface and into the client's consciousness, i.e. supressed and/or negative emotions and/or memories.
This can be quite an emotional process for the client and as a healer, you should be capable of assisting the client through this process or where necessary, recommend the client seek counselling.

For the client to feel secure and at ease with you, you need to connect with the client on a professional and non-judgemental level.

Listen

Sometimes we have a habit of hearing what someone is saying, but we do not listen to what is really being said. Disregard all your preconceived ideas and be open to what the client is saying. Also pay attention to the manner in which the person's words are conveyed to you.

Body Language

Your body language as a healer is important, as everybody reads and/or responds to body language on some level. Your body language needs to show your openness and you need to maintain eye contact with the client. Your client should feel at ease with you and be able to trust you.

Jargon

Do not use language, words and/or terms that the client will not be able to understand, as this creates confusion and emotional distancing.

Name

Ensure to use the client's name often when responding to him or her, as this shows the client that they have your full attention.

Personal Issues

Remember that the healing session is about your client and assisting an empowering him or her to heal. You should never discuss any personal issues with your client. In order to remain focused (and neutral) during a healing session, it is important to centre and ground your energy prior to the session.

Listen

Image obtained from Pixabay (September 2016)

Ensure to encourage a client to seek professional help, in the event that he or she may be in need of psychological or psychiatric assistance – although you can offer support you your clients, you need to be trained in Clinical Care.

Energy Exchange

Charging for Reiki

There has been an ongoing debate about the concept of "energy exchange" or charging for any healing modality. (This debate still continues today, without much resolve).

It is said that Mikao Usui (after doing much work in the poorest areas of Kyoto) encouraged an exchange for healing, in order to empower the client, by actively taking part in their healing process.

The story tells that he felt that anything "given free of charge is not valued". There should be some form of energy exchange – either in cash, in service or in kind, in return for Reiki healing.

Healing is universal and available to all, regardless of their financial status. However, as a Practitioner you may charge for your time, which has authenticated and clear value.

In today's world, in terms of "energy exchange", money can be seen as a direct extension of the time and energy that we put into our work. When a client wishes to have your time (your energy), they would have to pay money (their energy) for it.

You may decide to charge a lesser fee or an alternative energy exchange, in the event that you receive a request for healing from a person who does not have the financial recourses. But this is your personal choice.

Some are of the opinion that healing is less effective, or that healing cannot take place where there is no energy exchange. However, this is contradictory to the spirit of Reiki and healing in general. But, you may consider your own opinion in this regard.

Every practitioner has their own views and beliefs relating to "energy exchange" and therefore, you need to allow Reiki to guide you and come to a conclusion that is acceptable to you.

Image obtained from Pixabay (September 2016)

Treating a Client with Reiki

Reiki Level 1 teaches the basic routine, for treating others with Reiki. However, in Level 2 we will cover a more professional and detailed treatment routine.

In Level 1 you were taught that the client would need to turn over, in order for you to channel reiki to the back part of the client's body (back of the chakras).

However, the ideal with Level 2 teachings is to encourage you to now channel reiki to the back of each chakra, without asking the client to turn over onto his or her stomach.

To channel reiki energy to the back of the chakras you have visualize the energy going through the body to the back of the specific chakra that you are working on.

You will soon notice that the more you practice reiki (after completing Level 1) you are able to draw and hold more energy. You will also be able to better control the energy and channel more energy to a client.

The standard hand positions to channel reiki to the back part of the client's body remains the same as used on the front part of the body – with the only exception that you will channel the reiki energy to the back of each chakra.

On average, a session can last from 1 hour to 1 hour and 15 minutes.

Preparing for the Treatment

- Clear the room, by using the Reiki symbols and ask you Guides and Angels to assist you in clearing the space.

- Draw the power symbol (Cho Ku Rei) on your palms, tap the palms three times, to activate Reiki energy. Then protect your energy, by sealing your seven main chakras – cup your hand and place it over the Chakra. *(Repeat this with each Chakra and lastly your Aura) As on Page 13.*

- Ground and centre your energy.

- Invite your client into the room and start with the interview and treatment record.

- Explain the procedure to the client and answer any questions he or she may have.

- Ask the client to make him or herself comfortable on the bed and to consciously set the intention to be open to receiving healing.

- Connect with the client by placing one hand on the client's shoulder and the other hand on his or her wrist (or elbow). Whilst you are doing this silently do your opening prayer. (Here you can set the intention for healing to take place).

- Smooth or un-ruffle the client's aura.
- Scan the body (either with your hands, a pendulum, or a clear quartz terminator).

- If necessary - remove negative or stagnant energy, using the scooping technique. You will need a candle for this.

  Remember not to use this method on a person with a very sensitive energy system. Also remember to fill the area with Reiki energy and to seal in the new energy.

- Proceed with the Reiki hand positions. Should you feel guided to do so, you may draw the Reiki symbols over any area you are guided to, or over each chakra. *Follow your intuition.*

- Should the need arise and you have available space, you may also beam energy to the client.

- After completing the treatment, seal in the energy by drawing the power symbol (Cho Ku Rei) over the client's Solar Plexus Chakra, then cocoon the aura.

- Ground the recipient's energy (whilst doing your closing prayer).

- Offer the client a glass of water and discreetly wash your hands.

- End the session by discussing it with the client and allowing him or her to give you feedback of their experience.

Remember to advise the client to increase his or her water intake for two days, following the treatment.

- See the client out and re-clear the room and centre and ground your energy.

To maintain good practice, we will review the standard hand positions for treating others, below.

Review

Standard Hand Positions – for Treating a Client

Position 1

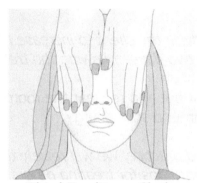

Third Eye/Brow Chakra

- Cup your hands and gently place your hands over the client's eyes. The palms should be directly over the eyes.
- If you are offering a treatment to someone who may not feel comfortable having their eyes covered, you may hold your hands just above their eyes.
- Eyes, face, nose, sinus, pituitary gland, stress, cerebellum.

- Self-awareness, perception, intuition, spiritual gifts, wisdom and higher consciousness.

Hold your hands in this position for three minutes, using your Reiki music (with the "three minute bell" to guide you when to change positions).

Position 2

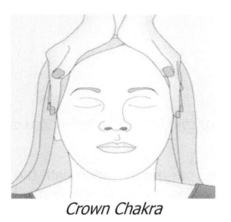

Crown Chakra

- Cup your hands and gently place your hands over the top (crown) of the client's head, your hands (on either side) with your fingers pointing towards the client's ears.
- Cerebellum, brain, skull, pineal gland.
- Balances the left and right hemispheres of the brain.
- Higher consciousness, spiritual centre, spiritual awareness.

Hold your hands in this position for three minutes.

Position 3

Back of the Third Eye/Brow Chakra

- Gently place your hands underneath the client's head. (As to allow the person to gently lay their head in your hands).
- Eyes, face, nose, sinus, pituitary gland, stress, cerebellum.
- Logic, the brain. Manifestation. To make your visualisation a reality.

Ensure to hold each position for three minutes, throughout the treatment session.

Position 4

Throat Chakra

- Gently place your hands on the sides of the client's face, with your fingertips touching at the client's chin.
- If the client is not comfortable having their face touched near the throat area, you may gently place your hands on either side at the collar bone area.
- Throat, neck, lungs, voice, vocal cords, thyroid gland, bronchioles, jaw.
- Expression, the ability to relate to others, contemplation, nourishment centre.

Position 5

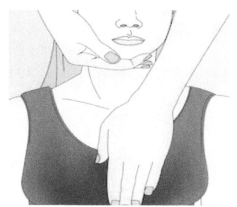

Throat Chakra/Heart Chakra

- Gently place your right hand underneath the client's chin and the left hand on the chest (on the Heart Chakra).
- If the client is not comfortable with these hand positions, you may hold both your hands just above the client's chest (over the Heart Chakra).
- You can also place your one hand on top of the other.
- Throat, neck, lungs, voice, vocal cords, thyroid gland, bronchioles, jaw.
- Heart, chest, ribcage, upper back, lower lungs abdominal cavity, thymus gland.
- Expression, the ability to relate to others, contemplation, nourishment centre.
- Balance, love, joy, compassion centre, surrender, respect.

- Working on the throat and heart chakra will assist the recipient in speaking their truth, but with a gentleness from the heart.

Position 6

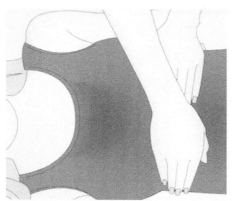

Solar Plexus Chakra

- Gently place your hands over the client's diaphragm area. Place your hands close together (with the one hand touching the other).
- Stomach, spleen, liver, abdomen, digestive system. Gall bladder, pancreas, autonomic nervous system and lower back.
- Self-expression, confidence, purpose, will power and shadow-self.

Position 7

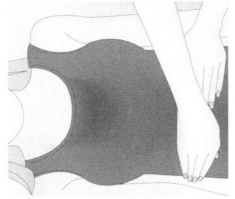

Sacral Chakra

- Gently place your hands over the client's navel area (slightly above the hip area) over the Sacral Chakra (which is located midway between your navel and the pelvic bone. (This is in the area where the reproductive organs are located).
- When offering a Reiki treatment to a male recipient, you may place your hands over the Sacral Chakra, just above the client's body.
- Bladder, pelvic area, reproductive organs, kidney, all fluids and liquids of the body.
- Creativity, polarity, pleasure, sexuality, sensuality and the inner child.

Position 8

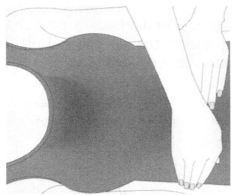

Root Chakra

- Position your hands slightly below the client's navel area (in the area of the hip bones) - *Keeping your hands just above the client's body* (In the area where the reproductive organs are located).
- Remember that the Reiki energy will be directed to the area where the Root Chakra is located (at the base of the spine).
- Legs, arms, feet, intestines, prostate, adrenal glands, rectum, anus, blood cells, bones, teeth and nails.
- Foundation, grounding, physical body, survival, vitality and solidity.

In order to proceed with reiki to the back part of the client's body, you may allow the client to turn over.

Or you may continue with the treatment – channelling the reiki energy from the front part of the body.

To proceed with reiki to the back of each chakra, you need to place your focus on channelling (sending) reiki energy to the back of each chakra.

The standard hand positions still apply with the exception that you have to channel (send) reiki to the back of each chakra.

Should you not feel comfortable using this technique yet, you may proceed with the standard hand positions below.

Position 9

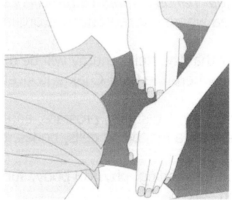

Back of the Heart Chakra

- Gently place your hands on the client's upper back (in the area just below the arm pits). This is the back of the Heart Chakra. Place the hands close together (with the one hand touching the other).
- Heart, chest, ribcage, upper back, lower lungs abdominal cavity, thymus gland.
- The ego/will and your ability to express yourself.

Position 10

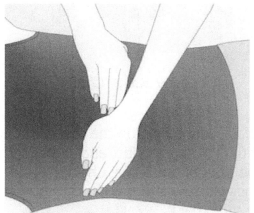

Back of the Solar Plexus Chakra

- Gently place your hands in the middle of the client's back (in the diaphragm area). Place the hands close together (with the one hand touching the other).
- Stomach, spleen, liver, abdomen, digestive system. Gall bladder, pancreas, autonomic nervous system and lower back.

- The intention of me and for me. How you perceive yourself.

Position 11

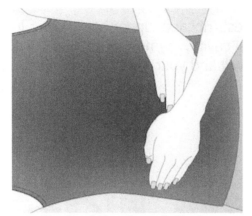

Back of the Sacral Chakra

- Gently place your hands on the client's lower back, at the navel area (just above the hips) – this is the back of the Sacral Chakra. Again, place your hands close together (with the one hand touching the other).
- Bladder, pelvic area, reproductive organs, kidney, all fluids and liquids of the body.
- Where you create pleasure in your life and the quantity of pleasure you create.

Position 12

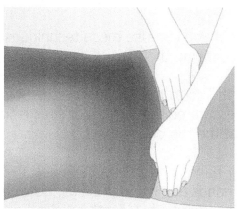

Back of the Root Chakra

- Gently place your hands on the client's lower back (at the base of the spine (just underneath the hip area). Again, place your hands close together (with the one hand touching the other).
- Legs, arms, feet, intestines, prostate, adrenal glands, rectum, anus, blood cells, bones, teeth and nails.
- Your sense of grounded-ness (feeling rooted). Your sense of survival.

After you have completed the treatment, remember to ground the client's energy.

You may do your closing prayer whilst doing this.

You may use one of the following grounding techniques.

Remember that you can use these techniques on their own or combine them.

- Use your thumb to press firmly on the Solar Plexus pressure point on the foot (this is just off the ball, at the top of the foot).

- Place your hands on the client's knees and gently pull your hands alongside the legs, down to the feet (do this swiftly, but gently) flicking off excess energy, as you get to the feet.

- Offer the client a glass of water or a biscuit.

- You can also allow the client to walk bare-feet.

- You can also allow the client to hold a crystal in their hand, but water or something to eat is the fastest way.

CHAPTER 7

Distant Healing

Distant Healing is a very effective method of sending Reiki healing to a recipient who is unable to receive the healing in person. Healing can be sent to anyone at any time anywhere in the world. Reiki energy is sent to the recipient by means of visualization.

How to Perform a Distant Healing

- Find a quiet place (where you will have no disturbances).
- Light a candle.
- Clear the room.
- Ask your Guides and Angels to assist you with the healing.
- Ground and centre your energy.
- Write the person's name on a piece of paper.
- Draw the Reiki symbols on the piece of paper - Hon Sha Ze Sho Nen, followed by Sei He Ki and then Cho Ku Rei.

- Beam Reiki energy to the person for a minimum of three minutes, or for as long as you may feel guided to do so.
- Say your closing prayer and give thanks for the healing.
- Then burn the piece of paper. By burning the piece of paper, you are releasing the healing to the recipient. (Do not dwell on the session).

There are also additional methods of performing Distant Healing. These are as follows:

- You may visualize yourself as the person you wish to send healing to and use your body as a surrogate. (As when doing a self-healing treatment).

- You may use a photograph of the person. Draw the Reiki symbols on the back of the photo and hold the photo in your hands and send Reiki energy.

- You may also use a teddy bear, a doll or a pillow as a surrogate. Send Reiki energy to the teddy bear or doll. In addition to healing, you may give the teddy bear to a child, as a gift.

- You may use your body as a surrogate, by using the left thigh - representing the front of the person's body and your right thigh as the back of the person's body.

- You may also send healing to a place on a map (or in a picture).

By sending distant healing, you also receive healing back. This also strengthens your connection with the divine.

CHAPTER 8

Chakra Affirmations

Sometimes we tend to underestimate our abilities and there are times when we do not take proper care of our bodies. There are also instances when we do not practice self-love and we may experience feelings of unworthiness.

Chakra Affirmations are an effective method to clear and balance the chakras. It encourages self-love, forgiveness and self-acceptance. It also brings about a feeling of balance, joy, positivity and a feeling of general wellbeing.

You may use chakra affirmations as part of or in addition to a Reiki treatment for a client, or you may use the chakra affirmations yourself.

Always start at the Root Chakra and work your way up to the Crown Chakra.

Root Chakra

- I trust in life's process.

- I trust that life will unfold for the greater good and my greatest sense of happiness.
- I know that I am worthy.
- I belong and I am safe.
- I am creative and my creativity can flourish.
- I play an integral part in the value of my life.
- My life is fulfilled and good.
- I am creating a healthy foundation for my life.
- I love my legs and my feet, they support me and show me the way.

Sacral Chakra

- I am enough.
- What I have and what I do is enough.
- I trust in life's processes.
- I allow sensuality, pleasure and sweetness into my life.
- I allow myself to be open to the joy, harmony and beauty that the universe has to offer.
- I trust in my own perfection and love myself as I am.

Solar Plexus Chakra

- I am worthy of self-love and respect.
- I listen to my deepest insights and trust my intuition.
- I do not judge myself.
- I allow my life to flow.
- There is no failure, only lessons.
- I learn from everything I do.

- I trust my worth and I am worth my weight in gold.

Heart Chakra

- I love and approve of myself.
- I believe and trust in love and open my heart to receiving love.
- I forgive myself.
- I feel complete.
- I am good, pure and innocent.
- I open my heart to the healing power of love.
- I follow the path of my heart.

Throat Chakra

- I express my feelings in a gentle manner.
- I am creative.
- I trust in my gifts.
- I express the best of who I am.
- I release doubt and fear, so I may express myself creatively.
- I am willing to take good care of myself at all times.
- I utilise my will power to control undesirable influences in my life.

Third Eye Chakra

- I open my intuition and deepest sense of knowing.
- I live truthfully in my beauty, grace and intelligence.

- I create boundless vision and clarity about my life.
- I am positive and think positively about everything that surrounds me.
- I trust that everything that crosses my path is in alignment with my greatest happiness and for my greater good.

Crown Chakra

- I am divinely guided and protected.
- I am surrounded, nourished and protected by love.
- I am open to receiving abundance from the universe.
- I acknowledge that love exists within me.
- I am safe, supported and loved.
- I am connected to life and to the universe.

CHAPTER 8

Healing with Color

Healing with colour does not traditionally form part of the original Usui Reiki teachings, but many practitioners incorporate colour into their healing practice.

You may choose to experiment with colour in your practice, but this depends on what you are comfortable with and the choice is entirely up to you.

The concept of incorporating colour into healing is based on the understanding that colour is light and it is the variation of light that creates the colour spectrum.
It is undeniable that colour holds positive energy and each colour in the spectrum possesses a unique frequency and association to energy.

Red

- The colour of the Root Chakra.
- This is a strong physical colour.
- It can stimulate energy and vitality.

- It generates warmth and heat.
- It is associated with the regeneration of cells and tissue.

Orange

- The colour of the Sacral Chakra.
- This colour helps one to adapt and digest life.
- It can be used to balance the emotional body.
- It is effective for healing unwillingness to forgive.
- It is effective for healing self-pity.

Yellow

- The colour of the Solar Plexus Chakra.
- This is a joyful colour.
- It is the life-giving colour of the sun.
- It is effective for healing the inner child.
- It can enhance the feeling of freedom to play and to have more fun.
- It can be effective to develop sensitivity rather than judgement.

Green

- The colour of the Heart Chakra.
- It is a soothing colour.
- It is well known as a healing colour.
- It balances and helps to develop unconditional love.

- It is effective for relieving fear of loving and possessiveness.
- It is the colour midpoint.

Blue

- The colour of the Throat Chakra.
- Effective for developing wisdom.
- It balances love and will.
- It inspires clarity, creativity and mental control.
- It eliminates confusion and encourages taking responsibility for others.

Indigo

- The colour of the Third Eye Chakra.
- It stimulates the intuition and imagination.
- This is an extremely spiritual colour.
- It can be used to expand the consciousness.

Purple

- The colour of the Crown Chakra.
- It is a colour of inspiration.
- It is the colour of change and transformation.
- It can be used to develop inspiration and spiritual awareness.

White

- The colour of the Stellar Gateway Chakra.
- This is a protective colour.
- It is also known as a colour of purity.
- It is the full light/colour spectrum in one.

- It enhances and energises the full energy system.

Image obtained from Pixabay (September 2016)

CHAPTER 8

Healing with Sound

It is believed by some that sound is the main building block of all existence.

Working with sound is not part of the original Usui Reiki teachings. However, some practitioners do incorporate this into their healing practice.

Should you decide to experiment with this, it can produce amazing results. But, once again this depends what you feel comfortable with and the choice is entirely up to you.

Reiki Circles

"Reiki Shares"

The nature of a reiki circle (reiki share) is similar to group healing, but it is different in the sense that it is more of a social and healing gathering of reiki practitioners.

Practitioners hold reiki circles, in order that they may share their experiences, support one another and give and receive reiki in a loving and honourable environment, amongst fellow practitioners (friends).

Attending reiki circles is an excellent method of gaining knowledge and practice. It aids reiki practitioners with self-growth and to honour each other as healers.

Much similar to a group healing, a number of healers will give reiki to one person and each practitioner has the opportunity to give and receive reiki at a reiki circle.

Additional Reiki Techniques

Traditional Techniques

Dry Bathing or Brushing Off (Kenyoku Hô)

Used to purify the body, heart and spirit

1. Stand in Gasshô position – ground and centre your energy and set the intention.

2. Arms at your sides - put your right hand on your left shoulder, with your fingertips touching the point where the collar-bone ends. Breathe in (through the nose) and as you breathe out intensely (through the mouth) move your hand diagonally across your body – from the left shoulder towards the right hip (use a smooth brushing action).

3. Arms at your sides - put your left hand on your right shoulder, with your fingertips touching the point where the collar-bone ends. Breathe in (through the nose) and as you breathe out intensely (through the mouth) move your hand diagonally across your body – from the right shoulder towards the left hip (use a smooth brushing action).

4. Lift your left arm (to form a straight horizontal line to the ground) palms facing down. Place your right hand on your left forearm. Breathe in (through the nose) and as you breathe out intensely (through the mouth) move your hand along the top of your left forearm sweeping all the way down over your fingertips.

5. Lift your right arm (to form a straight horizontal line to the ground) palms facing down. Place your left hand on your right forearm. Breathe in (through the nose) and as you breathe out intensely (through the mouth) move your hand along the top of your right

forearm sweeping all the way down over your fingertips.

6. Return to Gasshô position and give thanks.

Seated Gasshô position

Image obtained from Pixabay (September 2016)

Method of Healing at the Navel (Heso Chiryô Hô)

The umbilical or mother connection – You may use this on yourself and on clients

1. Sit or stand in Gasshô position – ground and centre your energy and set the intention.
2. Place your dominant hand flat over your navel and place your other hand in line with the navel, on your lower back.
3. Maintain this position until you feel balanced.
4. Return to Gasshô position and give thanks.

Method of Sending Ki with the Breath (Koki Hô)

May be used when a hands-on technique is not possible

1. Sit or stand in Gasshô – ground and centre your energy and set the intention.
2. Breathe in deeply through the nose and focus on the Hara Line – fill the lungs with reiki energy.
3. Blow the reiki energy out through the mouth (with your mouth in an "O" shape).
4. Return to Gasshô position and give thanks.

Additional Reiki Techniques

Non-Traditional Techniques

Connecting with the Reiki Symbol Energy (Symbol Meditation)

Meditation can strengthen your connection with Reiki energy

1. Stand in Gasshô – ground and centre your energy and set the intention.

2. Take a deep breath into the Sacral Chakra – follow the breath until you feel focused.

3. Draw the power symbol (Cho Ku Rei) in front of you. Visualize white light emanating from your fingers and the symbol being imprinted in the air.

4. Focus on this image and hold it in your mind, say its name three times. You may hold this image for as long as you wish.

5. Then visualize the symbol rising up above you and draw it down into your Crown Chakra.

6. Repeat this process with the mental/emotional symbol (Sei He Ki) and the distance symbol (Hon Sha Ze Sho Nen).

7. Return to Gasshô position and spend a few moments with the energy of reiki. Visualize a white cloud of reiki energy surrounding and enveloping your entire body.

This meditation energizes and charges you. After having done this meditation, it is a very favourable time to manifest your goals and/or practice distant healing.

Cleansing an Aura or Space with Smudging (Smudging)

The vibration of smell can effect changes in energy

1. Stand in Gasshô – ground and centre your energy and set the intention.

2. Protect your energy (as on Page 13). This is vitally important if you are cleansing someone else's house.

3. Use a smudge stick or incense. (White sage is well known for its cleansing properties).

4. Draw the power symbol (Cho Ku Rei) and say its name three times.

5. Start at the door and draw the infinity symbol in front of you, then at the top and all the way down to the floor.

6. Then move to the closest corner and draw the infinity symbol in front of you, then at the top and all the way down to the floor.

7. Repeat this in every corner. Then stand in the centre of the room and draw the infinity symbol in front of you.

8. Return to Gasshô position. Ground and centre your energy and give thanks.

Burning Incense

Image obtained from Pixabay (September 2016)

You may use this technique to clear every room/area of a house and then ground and centre your energy when you are done.

This technique can be used when you are moving into a new home or apartment. It can also be used to cleanse business properties/ factories etc.

CHAPTER 9

Manifestation

This technique was introduced into reiki by the western Usui/Tibetan Reiki Practitioners. This is a useful and effective technique to manifest things that you want or need.

However, it is important to remember that manifestation works in line with the universal laws of "co-creation" and "the greater good".

The following manifestation technique was derived from the original technique, but has been altered/adapted and incorporates a few different modalities.

Crystal Manifestation Grid

A crystal manifestation of your dreams

You will need:

Nine crystals

A canvas board or plywood or a wooden gift box

Glue / decorations / glitter (whatever you wish to use)

- Create a grid plate (as per the diagram below).
- Decorate your grid in any way you wish.

The grid will consist of nine numbered squares. This is based on numerical sequencing and on I-Ching. When you add the squares in a vertical, horizontal or diagonal direction, it adds up to fifteen. This is then reduced to six (1+5=6).

When creating your manifestation grid, the first thing to add onto your list, should always be "perfect health". You should reinstate your manifestation every 48 to 72 hours.

Always keep "co-creation" and "the greater good" in mind.

You must decide what you wish to manifest. Make a list of nine aspects of what you wish to create in your life. Number a page from 1 to 9.

Remember... number 1 on your list should always be "perfect health".

Example of a Manifestation Grid

Always ensure that your intentions are clear and pure!

Choosing and placing your crystals on the grid

- Pick one of your nine crystals that represents that which you wish to manifest. (Pay attention to what feels right).

- Programme each crystal – with emotion, not your thoughts. Warm the crystal in your hands, hold it over your heart chakra and third eye and state your intention. Visualize your goal and send that visualization from your heart to the crystal.

- *Be very clear in what you wish to manifest, to ensure that you get exactly what you wish for.*

- Once the crystal has been programmed, place the crystal on its designated number on the grid. (According to the numbers 1 to 9 on your list).

- *Do not glue the crystals to the grid!* **Use an alternative method to secure them, so you may remove and/or replace them, once the specific goal has been fulfilled.**

- Work with your grid as often as possible. Remember to keep your intentions clear and continue to restate your desires. Work diligently towards assisting the crystal to manifest your goals.

Examples of what you may manifest:

- To have a successful practice
- To travel to a specific country
- To find your dream home

Important points about Manifestation

- Do not manifest for other people.

- Do not manifest from your brain, but from your heart.

- Be very specific in what you want to manifest.

- Be cautious how you manifest.

- Remember that intention is key!

- Remember "co-creation" and "the greater good" – You have to co-create.

Image obtained from Pixabay (September 2016)

CHAPTER 10

Psychic Development

There are by and large six psychic "senses" which a person can experience.

- Clairvoyance – to clearly see.

- Clairaudient – to clearly hear.

- Clairalience – to clearly smell.

- Clairgustance – to clearly taste.

- Clairsentience – to clearly feel or sense.

- Claircognizant – to clearly know or understand.

In French, "clair" is a suffix, which means clear or clearly.

Image obtained from Pixabay (September 2016)

Psychic Sensory Terminology

Psychometry

This is the ability to touch an object and pick up on psychic impressions, left on the object by vibrations.

Empathic

This is the ability to sense the emotions, needs and drives of others. To pick up feelings and emotions, based on the mental and physical energies, which a person gives off.

Precognition

This is the ability to know and/or look into the future before it takes place.

Telepathy

This is the ability to sense what another person is thinking.

Medium

This is the ability to hear or see spirits.

There are many people who are aware of and "in tune" with all of these senses. However, most people only focus on developing one or two.

Although developing these additional senses may offer valuable insight into a reiki session, it is not compulsory and it will in no way have any influence on the effectiveness or purity of reiki.

Developing your Psychic Senses

Developing these additional psychic senses can be as easy or as difficult as you perceive it to be. The key factor in developing these senses is "trust".

You would need to surpass the logical mind and find a sense of deep-seated trust in the higher consciousness.

There is no method of teaching anyone to "tune into" these senses. As in self-growth and development, it is a personal process of acceptance, discovery and trust.

In order to connect with your higher self or to enhance your energetic perception, keep the following in mind.

Know thyself

Continue on your path of self-discovery, self-acceptance and self-awareness. (Get to really know yourself).

Awareness

Be more self-aware and aware of your surroundings.

Dreams

Keep note of your dreams. As you grow in awareness, it will be easier to remember your dreams. Dreams have always been seen as a doorway to the subconscious.

Listen

Truly listen to the world, not only the words and sounds, but pay attention to the manner in which they are conveyed. Recognize the inter-connectedness of the universe and all in it.

Pay attention

Pay attention to your thoughts and feelings and look for patterns that may surface.

Silence and Solitude

We all need "quiet time" in solitude. Make this a time to reflect and connect to your personal energy and the energy of the universe.

CONCLUSION

Final Thoughts

- Remember to follow your intuition.
- Remember that intention is key.
- Remember to practice channelling (sending) reiki to the back of each chakra – practice makes perfect.
- Remember to use techniques which you feel most comfortable with.
- There is no right or wrong way of doing a reiki treatment, reiki energy will do what it needs to do and go where it needs to go.
- Remember that each client will experience their reiki treatment session differently and this is normal.
- Remember that you may design and/or use your own "Client Information Form" – But, remember to insert a **"Disclaimer"**.
- Enjoy the journey and enjoy the process.

Once you have been attuned to reiki, it will always be a part of you, whether you studied reiki for self-growth only, or wish to open your own practice.

Each Reiki Master, student/practitioner has his or her own unique gift. Those who require your gift will be guided to find you.

Now that you have completed Reiki Level 2 - Enjoy this wonderful gift of sharing Reiki with others.

I wish you much love and light on your journey!

Treatment Record
Example of a Client Information Form

CLIENT INFORMATION FORM

Date of Treatment:
Name:
Surname:
Date of Birth:
Contact Tel. Number:
Contact E-mail Address:
Expectations of Treatment:

Medical Conditions:

Areas of concern:

Additional Information:

I have completed the above medical history and agree that the information provided here is a true record. I have not withheld any information that may affect the course of my treatment. It is my decision to have this treatment and I know that the therapist may not diagnose or prescribe. I agree to seek professional medical care for any medical conditions. If undergoing any treatment, I agree to inform the practitioner that I am receiving this treatment(s) in addition to their care.

Signed by Client:
Date signed:

For pratctioner's use:-
Notes / Comments:
Follow up date:
Notes / Comments:

Developing your Reiki Practice
Article by William Lee Rand

This article can be located on William Rand's website:
http://www.reiki.org/reikipractice/practicehomepage.html

Reiki is a truly wonderful gift and while some take Reiki training to use on themselves and with friends and family, many feel inspired to share it with a much wider circle. The development of a Reiki practice can be a very rewarding experience. Not only can it provide you with a source of income, there are spiritual experiences that can be much more meaningful.

So, assuming you have been initiated into Reiki and have the ability to channel Reiki healing energy to others, I would like to share some ideas and techniques that may be helpful in developing a Reiki practice.

Intention is the Most Important Thing

The most important thing concerning the development of a Reiki practice is the quality and strength of your intention. The mind is like a magnet. The quality and strength of your thoughts will determine the quality and strength of what you attract into your life. Therefore it is important for you to develop and maintain a positive mental attitude about your Reiki practice.

Decide with clarity, determination and commitment that you are going to create a thriving Reiki practice. Decide that you are worthy to do this and that there are many people who will benefit from your service. Decide that the value you and your clients will receive from your Reiki practice will far outweigh any effort or sacrifice that might be involved in creating it. Picture in your mind the results you want to create and how it will feel when you are actively involved in a thriving Reiki practice.

Meditate frequently on this image and these feelings. Allow them to fill you up and surround you and reach out to others. Use this to motivate you and to help you continue on in the face of doubt or discouragement. Know in your heart that the freedom, joy and satisfaction of having your own Reiki practice is a valid goal and that you are creating it. Believe in yourself and in your purpose.

If doubts arise about your goal, know that this is normal and assume that they have entered your consciousness because they are passing out of you. Whenever we take on a new level of healing or commit to a new goal, old negative thoughts and feelings that have been stored inside and have gone unchallenged are dislodged and begin moving through our consciousness.

If your commitment is strong, these old negative feelings and thoughts will break up and be released. If you feel negative feelings and thoughts come up, know that this is part of your healing and that you are releasing them up to the Higher Power to be healed. Use your Reiki to speed this up and make sure to ask for treatments from others. Reiki psychic surgery can be especially helpful.

Compassion Brings Help From Higher Sources

There are higher sources of help you can call on. Angels, beings of light and Reiki spirit guides as well as your own enlightened self are available to help you. They can help you develop your Reiki practice by directing clients to you and assisting with treatments. They can be of great benefit, but you must have a strong spiritual intention for your work if you are to recruit their aid.

If you are doing Reiki in a selfish way, only for money or to gain control over others or to take on an air of self-importance, or for any other negative purpose, then it will be very difficult for these spiritual beings to work with you. There must be congruence, an alignment within you in order for the Higher Power in the form of Reiki to flow through you in a powerful way and in order for the angels, Reiki spirit guides and other spiritual beings to work with you.

Reiki wants only the best for you, but you must align with the nature of Reiki if you are to gain the greatest benefit. The more you can open to the true nature of Reiki which is to have an unselfish heart centred desire to help others, then the more the Reiki spirit guides can help you. Focus on helping others and on healing anything within yourself that may stand in the way of an uninhibited flow of love and compassion. This is what will make your Reiki practice a success!

The development of a spiritual attitude toward your Reiki practice can be facilitated through the regular use of affirmations and prayers. Try the following prayer: "Guide me and heal me so that I can be of greater service to others." By sincerely saying a prayer such as this each day, your heart will open and a path will be created to receive the help of higher spiritual beings. They will guide you in your Reiki practice and in the development of your life purpose.

Competitiveness is Not a Part of Reiki

One thing that can get in the way of developing a spiritual attitude about your Reiki practice is fear of competition. This has caused more problems and created more restrictions and negative energy in the Reiki community than any other area of misunderstanding. Lack is an illusion and this is especially true for Reiki!

There is a far greater need for healing on the planet than there are Reiki practitioners who can provide it. Fear of competition goes directly against the nature of Reiki energy and because of this, it can repel people from you who might otherwise be interested in receiving a treatment. Reiki comes from an unlimited supply and does not fear competition.

People who do Reiki together find that their Reiki gets stronger as more people join the group. If Reiki was competitive, then just the opposite would happen, it would be strongest when you were alone and get weaker as more people joined the group. The nature of Reiki energy is one of cooperation. It understands the concept that we are all one and flows freely to anyone and everyone. It works in harmony with all other forms of treatment. It is clearly apparent, the wisdom of Reiki is to welcome all other practitioners as allies. If the spiritual purpose for your

Reiki practice, is to help others and to heal the planet, then you can only rejoice when you hear about another Reiki practitioner in your area as they are helping you fulfil your purpose.

Accept the wisdom of Reiki as your own wisdom, that all others who practice Reiki are helping you. The more you can do this, the more your Reiki practice will thrive. Don t worry about taking clients away from other practitioners. Each practitioner has their own value and special way of helping others. You will attract the clients who are right for you. Others will attract the clients who are right for them.

Reiki Will Soon Be in Great Demand

An important trend is developing in society that will soon create a great demand for Reiki practitioners. More and more people are discovering the value of alternative therapy. A recent study conducted by Dr. David M. Eisenberg of Boston s Beth Israel Hospital indicates that people in the US are beginning to turn away from modern medicine and make greater use of alternative health care techniques.

The survey concluded that 34 percent of Americans said they used at least one alternative therapy in 1990 and that Americans are spending nearly $14 billion a year for this treatment, most of which comes out of the patients own pocket. The therapies most used are meditation, touch therapy (such as Reiki), guided imagery, spiritual healing, chiropractic, hypnosis, homeopathy, acupuncture, herbal cures, and folk remedies.

Also of note is the fact that the National Institutes of Health has created an Office of Alternative Medicine whose purpose is to research alternative healing methods and establish their value. Already many healing techniques formerly considered quackery by the medical establishment have been proven valid by this new office.

These include chiropractic, acupuncture and homeopathy and they will soon be studying touch therapy and Reiki. Clearly, a paradigm shift is taking place toward the general acceptance of alternative medical treatment. It is likely that Reiki will become widely accepted as a valid form of healing before the end of the decade! Think what this means for anyone with a Reiki practice. A great need is developing for Reiki practitioners!

The Practical Issue of Money

Now that we have covered some of the important attitudes, values and beliefs necessary for a thriving Reiki practice, let's discuss some of the practical issues. An important issue is money. Some practitioners do not charge money and this is fine if that is their decision as everyone has the right to charge whatever they want or to charge nothing at all.
However, it is often better for the client if they are able to give something in return. They are not paying for the Reiki energy which is free but for your time and the effort you have put forth to learn Reiki.

When people receive a treatment for free they often feel indebted to the practitioner and guilty feelings can develop. This creates an imbalance that can get in the way of continued treatments. Charging money allows people the freedom to come whenever they want. If you do have clients who have a money problem, you can charge them less or barter.

How much should you charge for a Reiki session? A good rule of thumb is to charge about the same for a standard Reiki session as others in your area are charging for massage. A standard Reiki session will usually last about 45 minutes to an hour and a half. When you first start charging for your sessions, you can start at a lower rate if that feels comfortable to you and increase it as your confidence and reputation grow.

Advertise Your Practice

Business cards are a good first step when starting your practice. They let people know you are serious about your Reiki business and make it easy for you to give people your phone number in case they want to make an appointment. It is not a good idea to place you address on the card as people may come without calling you.

It is a good idea to talk to people first to get a feel for their energy, and let them know what they can expect from a Reiki session before setting up an appointment and giving them directions to your home or office.

Flyers are also a good idea. In your flyer explain what Reiki is and the benefits it offers along with your name and phone number. You can place them on bulletin boards in health food stores and new age book stores etc. and they can be given out to prospective clients.

Beginning your Reiki practice from your home is a good idea as it will save money on start-up costs, but many practitioners have found advantages to having their own office. An office creates a professional atmosphere and lets people know that you take your work seriously.

You may want to start in your home and get an office after things get going or if you can afford it, get an office right away. Consider the fact that you may want to have group activities in your office when considering the size office you want.

Make sure to get each client's name address and phone number for your mailing list. As your list grows, you can mail out flyers on upcoming Reiki events or simply remind people about your practice. A good way to keep track of your clients is to use a client information form. The one in the back of "Reiki, The Healing Touch" is a good one as it includes a disclaimer which protects you from misunderstandings about the results you promise from a Reiki session.
Feel free to make copies of this form and use it in your practice. Keep your mind open to other ways of adding people with an interest in alternative healing to your mailing list. The mailing list can be an important tool in promoting your Reiki practice.

Exchange Treatments

One way to let people know about your Reiki practice is to offer to exchange Reiki with other alternative therapists. This works well with massage therapists as they are familiar with body work and often need therapy themselves. Offer to refer clients to them and ask them to do the same for you. Give them some of your flyers or business cards to display in their office.

Give Impromptu Demonstrations

When you are at public gatherings or around others and someone complains about an ache or pain, offer to give them Reiki. If they have never heard of Reiki before, explain that it is a Japanese form of stress reduction with many healthy benefits. If they have a metaphysical understanding you can talk about Ki and the life force etc.

Talk to them on a level they can understand. Take 15 minutes or so to treat the area of concern and let them know you do this professionally and give them your card. Tell them what a complete session is like and set up an appointment if they are interested.

At parties or large gatherings, the attention you attract when giving Reiki to one often creates interest in others who will want a sample treatment also. Often you end up treating several people and passing out many business cards. As you treat you can talk about Reiki and how it works. Ask the person to explain what they feel. This always creates a lot of interest.

Being focused on helping the person and not on getting a client is the key to attracting people for sample treatments. However, if they are interested, a business card is appropriate.

One thing that will really attract attention for your Reiki practice is wearing a Reiki T-shirt. People will want to know what the symbols mean and this opens the door to talking about Reiki. Offer to give them a sample treatment and telling them about your practice. If they seem interested, give them a business card and if possible, setup an appointment.

Offer Free Reiki Evenings

A free Reiki evening can create lots of interest. Plan one night a month to talk about Reiki and give sample treatments. If you have Reiki friends, ask them to come and help give treatments. This is a great way to help others and let them know about Reiki and your practice. Make up flyers for your free Reiki evening and put them up in appropriate places.

If the Reiki practitioners can meet an hour or so before the meeting to give treatments to each other it will really improve the quality of what the non-Reiki people receive. Also, if you have taken Reiki III\master training, you could give a refresher attunement or healing attunement to each of the practitioners to boost their energy. This is a great way for the practitioners to practice their Reiki and for you to practice giving attunements. Call everyone you know who would be interested and let them know.

If your area has psychic or holistic fairs, get a booth. Take a Reiki table and ask 5 or more of your Reiki friends to help. Offer 10 or 15 minute treatments with 5 or more Reiki practitioners giving a treatment to one person at a time. Charge $10.00 or so per treatment. This can be a powerful healing experience and a good demonstration of Reiki.

Have a table with your flyers and business cards on it and be sure to get each person's name, address, and phone number for your mailing list. Another way is to use chairs and have one or two practitioners give 10 or 15 minute treatments to each person. The chair method takes up less space and allows you to treat more than one person at a time.

Offer Reiki as a Public Service

Create a healing service at your church. Recruit other healers to help. You could use both Reiki and non-Reiki healers. This can create tremendous interest in Reiki. Refer to the Summer 93 issue of the Reiki News for a complete explanation.

Volunteer to do free Reiki treatments at hospitals, hospice centres, drug and alcohol treatment centres or in conjunction with a psychologist or other therapists. By doing this, you will gain experience and people will find out about your practice, but most of all, you will be helping others.

If there is a metaphysical/holistic paper in your area, offer to write an article for it on Reiki or healing in general. Make sure your name and phone number are listed and that you are a Reiki practitioner or teacher. If you are really serious, decide to write an article every month.

This will let people know who you are and what your attitudes and beliefs are concerning healing. They will then be able to decide if they want to come to you. It is also a good idea to place an ad in the same paper your article appears in. You will pay for the ad, but the article will be free!

Write articles for the Reiki News or send in a description of your Reiki experiences. The Reiki News needs articles and is very interested in letting people know about your personal experiences with Reiki. It goes out to thousands of people interested in Reiki all over the country. Having your name in the paper will improve your reputation especially if you place free copies in your local health and new age book stores and hand out copies to your clients and friends etc.

Deliver Talks on Reiki

Develop a Reiki talk and offer to speak about Reiki to local groups. There are many groups looking for speakers and alternative healing is becoming a hot topic. If you have little experience at public speaking, you can join a local Toast Masters Club. There you will be coached and given ample opportunity to develop your speaking ability. If you are making Reiki your career, then the ability to speak before groups is a must. Decide to become a great speaker and go for it.

Cultivate the Media

In many parts of the country the news media are reporting the positive benefits of alternative healing. So, call the local newspapers and TV stations. Find out which reporter(s) are in charge of or interested in information about alternative healing. Talk to them and let them know you are a Reiki practitioner/teacher. Explain Reiki to them in a way they can understand - tell them it is a Japanese form of stress reduction and relaxation that can also facilitate healing.

Tell them there are over 100,000 practitioners in the US and the numbers are growing! Give them details and make it interesting and exciting. Offer to give them a free treatment. Let them know that you are available should they decide to write an article or air a program about Reiki or alternative healing or if any questions come up about it in the future.

Establish in their mind that you are an expert on Reiki. They will then think of you as a resource person. Most reporters keep a file of people they can call on for different subjects and they will probably put your name in it! If they are not ready to do a story now, when they are ready, it is likely they will call you!

Become Licensed through the Centre

Become certified as a Reiki Master/Teacher by the Centre. When you do this, we will list your classes in the newsletter and refer students and clients to you. The Centre continually receives requests from people from all over the country who are interested in Reiki sessions and classes. If you are certified by the Centre, we can then refer these prospective clients to you.

If you are beginning to teach and are having trouble getting a class together, simply plan a class, set a date and assume the class will be full. Then when you tell people about the class, they will pick up a positive attitude from you about the class and want to come. If people sense a tentativeness, it will discourage them from attending.
Being decisive about your plans and having a positive attitude will attract students and bring the class together. Your guides will also be better able to work with you if you are clear about what you intend to do.

These ideas have worked for others, they will work for you. Try them! Also, use your intuition to develop other ways to promote your Reiki practice. Remember, a clear intention is the first step to success. Keep track of the result you get with each thing you try.

Keep using the ones that work and drop the ones that don't. Keep trying new things until you get the results you want. By following this formula you will create a successful Reiki practice and in so doing, bring joy, peace and healing to others.

Interesting References

Once one opens up to the concept that "all is energy" and you commence with studies such as Reiki Healing, it opens up to us a cosmic journey of growth, self-love, self-acceptance and ultimately self-healing.

There are various books and resources available, offering valuable insight and information about Reiki and energy.

Below is a list of books you may find resourceful.

The Essence of Reiki 2 – Usui Level 2 Advanced Practitioner Manual

Adele & Gary Malone

This is a step by step guide to the teachings and disciplines associated with Second Degree Usui Reiki. Follow the link below:

https://www.amazon.com/Essence-Reiki-Practitioner-disciplines-associated-ebook/dp/B0091GZJOG/ref=asap_bc?ie=UTF8#nav-subnav

The Spirit of Reiki

W. Lubeck, F. Arjava Petter & W. Rand

Hands of Light

Barbara Ann Brennan

The Reiki Source Book

Bronwen & Frans Steine

Light Emerging

Barbara Ann Brennan

Wheels of Light

Rosalyn Bruyere

On your journey of self-discovery and self-healing, you may also find the following books helpful.

A Step in the Right Direction – Daily Devotional

Jennifer Rossouw

(A spiritual devotional with inspirational messages for each day of the year)

The Alchemist

Paulo Coelho

(About learning the language of the universe)

The Teachings of Lao Tzu – The Tao Te Ching

Translated by Paul Carus

(A valuable guide about the teachings of Lao Tzu)

Angel Therapy

Doreen Virtue Ph.D.

(This book is a valuable guide through difficult times)

Sixth Sense

Stuart Wilde

(This book is a valuable guide to using your intuition)

The Crystal Bible Volume 1

Judy Hall

(A valuable guide to over 200 crystals) – Although there are later versions available today

Your Body Speaks Your Mind

Deb Shapiro

(About the association between body and mind)

Made in United States
North Haven, CT
24 June 2023